THE FOURTH BOOK OF CURRIES

Also written by Harvey Day
and published by Nicholas Kaye

CURRIES OF INDIA
THE SECOND BOOK OF CURRIES
THE THIRD BOOK OF CURRIES

ACKNOWLEDGMENTS

I should like to thank all who have helped me, especially Mrs May Ewing, formerly of Kanchrapara, in the Twenty Four Perghannas, Bengal, *cordon bleu* in the curry world; and also Mrs Yvette Loos for her recipes of Singhalese curries. Without their aid I would have been like an astronaut trying to land on the dust-bowls of the Moon.

My thanks go out to all my readers who have written appreciative letters; and to the doubtless many more who have passed away after sampling my recipes. These were like disciples of the Flat Earth theory—they've fallen over the edge and can't return to accuse me.

Dorchester-on-Thames   H.D.
Oxon.

THE FOURTH BOOK OF CURRIES

by

HARVEY DAY

Drawings by B. Gerry

NICHOLAS KAYE

LONDON

First published by
NICHOLAS KAYE LIMITED
194–200 Bishopsgate, London, E.C.2
1964

Printed in England by
ADLARD AND SON LIMITED
London and Dorking

Contents

CHAPTER ONE

Idle Thoughts on Curry

THERE are some who can't abide curry. I know a man, apparently civilized, who says, 'Give me a plate of corned beef and chips and you can keep your curry—or caviar!' There is no accounting for tastes. The Eskimo delights in *muk-tuk*, which is rancid blood and blubber mixed with putrefying fish.

Perhaps the idea persists that Indian cooks are dirty and their dishes permeated by disease germs, but in India cooking is a rite and before a Hindu lady enters her kitchen, she bathes and puts on clean clothing. The spices in which foods are curried have antiseptic value; and the *Sustras* lay it down that naught shall be eaten unless it has a protective skin or shell; that vegetables must not be left over from one meal to the next; and that onions, which harbour germs when peeled, shall be eaten at one sitting, unless curried.

Cooling and Heating Properties of Food

In India the temperature may vary in different parts, from 110°F. in the shade to below zero; so as you journey from place to place, you hear men discussing the 'cooling' and 'heating' properties of foods.

What they mean is that some foods induce a feeling of coolness in the body, whereas others appear to warm it. Steaming tea and pungent curries are cooling because they make you perspire; coffee, wheaten products, lentils, milk and all flesh have a heating effect. Europeans, who eat them to excess, get prickly heat; Indians rarely do.

Infinite Variety

Curries vary in areas where people speak different languages or dialects, and there are some dozen official languages and some 300 or more dialects in India and Pakistan. There is an infinite variety of curries, on which subject I shall touch later. According to the *Sustras* and the *Code of Manu*, meals should be planned to whip up the appetite, maintain it, and finally aid digestion. Curries convey richness and taste, rice softens the pungency, and so on. The cardamoms and cloves which finish off a meal cleanse the breath and help digestion too. Each dish should be complementary to the others and play its part in the general scheme.

Salt

Salt is meant to flavour, not poison, food. Far too much is eaten. Dr Victor Heiser says that Americans eat half an ounce of salt a day; the British consumption is *one tablespoon* a day! Medical experts say that too much salt aggravates many diseases, increases high blood pressure, coronary disease and constipation; and Professor Coirault, the famous French neuro-psychiatrist, has proved that when too much salt is eaten the body finds it difficult to rest and insomnia is the result.

CHAPTER TWO

Miscellaneous Hints

A Word about Fats

Ghee is clarified butter; that is, butter treated with steam to remove impurities. It tastes different from butter, and once used for cooking will always be preferred.

When mustard oil is used, it must always be heated till a wisp of blue smoke rises from its surface before putting ingredients into it. It is extremely digestible, like olive oil; but make sure you have the grocer's, not the chemist's brand!

For the best results, use ghee, butter, mustard oil or olive oil; but lard, dripping, sessamum, peanut, coconut or soya-bean oil are all permissible. If you find the quantities given make the food too rich, experiment with less.

Curry Ingredients

SPICES

INDIAN NAME	ENGLISH NAME	BOTANICAL NAME
souf	aniseed	*Pimpinella Anisum*
seetul	allspice	*Myrtus Pimenta*
eelachie	cardamom	*Elelbaria Cardamomum*
jawatrie	mace	*Myristica Moschata*
jauphull	nutmeg	*Myristica Moschata*
kulmie darchini	cinnamon	*Laurus Cinnamonum*
dhunnia or *kotimear*	coriander	*Doriandrum Sativum*
laoong	cloves	*Engenia Caryophyllata*
zeera or *jeera*	cummin seed	*Cummin Cyminum*
kala mirchi	black pepper	*Piper Nigrum*
rai	mustard seed	*Sinopis Chinesis*
lal mirchi	chillis	*Capsicum Frutescens*

huldie	turmeric	Curcuma Longa
maythi	fenugreek	Trigonella Foenum Craecum
lassoon	garlic	Alium Sativum
sont	ginger (dry)	Amomum Zingiber
udruck	ginger (green)	Amomum Zingiber
khush-khush	poppy seed	Papaver Somniferum
pipel	long pepper	Piper Longum
hing	asafoetida	Ferula Asafoetida
chironji	chironji nut	Buchanonia Latifolia
badam	almond	Amygdalia Communis
nareul	coconut	Cocus Nufifera
keori or kevara	screw-pine	Pandanus odoratissimus

In addition to these, yogurt, coconut milk or cream, tamarind, and special legumes such as *channa* and *mussoor* are used in certain curries. Yogurt may be bought at many dairies, or it can be made at home. Tamarind and the pulses may be bought at shops that specialize in Indian spices (see page 62), and so may coconut milk or cream. But if preferred, this may be made at home.

The Indian method is to split a coconut in half and scrape away the flesh with a special grater. Place it in a saucepan with a large cup of water, and bring to the boil. Simmer for a minute, then pour into a stout china bowl and mash with a heavy spoon. Strain the liquor before use. This is known as 'thick milk'.

If the flesh is subjected once more to the same process—that is, boiled and strained, the liquid is known as 'thin milk'.

Another method is to mix or mash desiccated coconut in boiling water and then strain through fine muslin. Use approximately 1 breakfast cup of coconut to $\frac{1}{2}$ pint of water.

Unless specifically instructed to do so, never place a lid on a saucepan in which a curry is being cooked with coconut milk, as the milk tends to curdle and the gravy turns lumpy.

In all the recipes given, the quantity of chilli has been reduced considerably, and if the curry is too pungent, it may be cut down still further. If curries have never been eaten before it is also advisable to discard the seeds of red chillis.

NOTE: Throughout the book the term 'spoon' implies a FLAT, not a heaped, spoonful.

CHAPTER THREE

The Function of Rice

In India, as elsewhere, there are many indiscriminate feeders; we do not base our standards on them but on the gourmets and epicures. We don't mix every article of food into one bowl on the principle that ultimately they will mingle in our stomachs, but keep them apart so that the various flavours may delight our palates. In Europe the French do this better than any nation; in Asia, the Indians.

It is generally understood that in India rice is meant to serve the purpose that bread or potatoes do in Britain, as a 'filler', but this is not quite so. Here, meat of various kinds imparts flavour, and bread and potatoes fill the vast empty spaces because they are bulkier and cheaper. In Italy spaghetti and macaroni do the same thing. At a well-planned Chinese dinner, rice is served last and it is a compliment to your host to confess that you are so full that you simply cannot touch it! This does not apply, of course, to the majority who are poor and depend on rice to fill their stomachs.

In India rice isn't supposed to be a filler, but a *neutral base* which helps to bring out the flavours of the various dishes. A little curry from one dish should be placed on an area of virgin rice; a little curry from another dish placed on another free area of rice; and so on. You sample one kind of curry with a little rice, then another, and another. If the curry is too pungent, a little more plain rice will subdue the burning pangs. It can be sweetened with chutney or given an acid tang with pickle.

Nutritional Value of Rice

The idea that plain white rice is coolie's food and that the well-to-do eat only *khichiri* or *pilau* is nonsense. Plain, well-cooked white rice, where every grain is separate, forms the base for some of the choicest meals. The best rice nutritionally is that from which the thin red skin—like that on the peanut—has not been removed. The red skin contains 17 I.U. (International units) of vitamin A, 15 I.U. of B_1

10

and 1.00% mineral matter; whereas polished (white) rice contains no vitamin A or B_1, and only 0.35% mineral matter.

Red rice is the staple food of the very poor, who, if they can afford it, add to rice a handful of lentils or a few vegetables. Those who can afford it eat pure (?) white rice, just as white bread, denuded of vitamins and minerals, is eaten by most people in Britain.

Plain Boiled Rice

Plain boiled rice is one of the easiest dishes to make. Wash the rice several times and drain away the water. Then three parts fill a large saucepan with water and bring it to the boil. Add a teaspoon of salt and sprinkle in the rice with one hand. Always use a great deal of water, for rice swells alarmingly. Boil *hard* for 10–12 minutes, then take out a few grains and test between finger and thumb. If necessary, cook a little longer. When rice is soft but *still firm*, take the pan off the flame, hold it under a tap and pour in cold water. This separates the grains from each other. Now strain into a sieve or colander. Then butter the bottom of a warm dish and shake the rice into it. Set the dish in a warm place, but not on a flame. In 10 minutes it will be fit for the table. One breakfast cup of rice is enough for 2 people.

This method is foolproof except for the most ham-handed. By following the directions, those who have hitherto turned out a gluey mess will produce a pile of firm, soft, snowy grains.

Alternative Method of Cooking Rice

Measure (with cups) the quantity of rice needed. Measure accurately twice the volume of water as of rice. Place rice and water in a thick-bottomed pan to soak for at least an hour.

Bring rice and water to the boil, then turn down flame and simmer on a very low flame till every particle of water has been absorbed. While simmering, cover with a well-fitting lid. The rice should be perfectly cooked and each grain separate when the last drop of water has evaporated.

TURKISH SHELLFISH PILAU

½ breakfast cup olive oil	10 medium-sized onions
2 breakfast cups rice	3 breakfast cups water
1 cup shelled mussels or	2 cups shelled oysters
1 cup scallops	3 teaspoons mixed herbs
a sprinkle of pepper	salt—to taste

Slice the onions finely and fry them to a golden colour in the oil. Put in the water and rice and bring them to the boil; then add the fish and green herbs and sprinkle liberally with pepper. Add salt, simmer gently till all water has evaporated, turn out into a flat dish and place in an oven preheated at 200 degrees F. Leave for ten minutes; then serve.

Enough for four.

PORK PILAU

1 breakfast cup of rice	1½ lb. lean, boned pork
6 bananas	½ lb. brown sugar (pieces)
1 inch of cinnamon (ground)	½ pint lemon juice *or*
4 bay leaves	½ pint apple cider vinegar
12 cloves (grind)	a generous pinch of basil
4 large onions, finely chopped	a generous pinch of origano
6 oz. butter	(wild marjoram)

Cut the pork into inch-pieces and brown in a smear of butter, together with onion and a squeeze of lemon juice. (Lime may be used if you wish.) When the pork is well browned, cover with water and boil till tender. Take the pan off the stove. Mix the sugar and lemon juice (or vinegar) in a small pan and cook till the mixture is thick, like syrup, and put aside the pan.

Place the rice, butter and bay leaves in a pan, add water till the level is an inch above the rice, and bring to the boil; then simmer. When the rice is ready (test by feeling individual grains), make a hollow in the mass, place the pork and chopped onions inside it, cover with rice and simmer for five minutes. Then turn into a large flat dish and place in a pre-heated oven (about 200°F.)

Now peel the bananas, split and cut them into pieces, roll them in flour, sprinkle with powdered cinnamon and cloves, pop them into the syrup and simmer for half an hour. Place them on top of the rice and pork, garnish with basil and origano and serve hot.

Enough for four.

RICE SURPRISE

1 breakfast cup of rice
½ cup fried bacon
3 onions, finely sliced
1 lb. of chicken pieces
½ lb. carrots
½ lb. peeled chestnuts
4 cloves garlic
a sprinkle of paprika
salt

6 chipolata sausages
½ cup Lancashire cheese
¼ cup Parmesan cheese *or*
  ½ cup Leicester cheese
2 tablespoons butter
a pinch of tarragon
a pinch of coriander
1 teaspoon jeera

Grill the chicken pieces till they are tender enough to eat. Prick the sausages with a fork and grill them, too. Cut the carrots into cubes and cook carrots and onions in just enough water to soften them. Put aside. Cook chestnuts, jeera and coriander in water and a little salt, and put aside.

Place rice, garlic, butter and tarragon in a pan, add any water left from cooking carrots and onions, or chestnuts, jeera, etc.; bring to the boil and then simmer till done.

Turn the rice into a large dish. Make a hollow in the middle, put the chicken pieces in, cover with rice, arrange sausages and bacon on top, then chestnuts, and heat for a minute or two. The rice should be dry, tender and steaming. Garnish with onions and carrots and sprinkle with the two kinds of cheese, which will add colour and flavour.

Alternatively, the cheese can be added to the carrots and onions, cooked for a few minutes and poured over the rice. If this is done, sprinkle with paprika.

Enough for four.

DUCK PILAU

1 duck
1 breakfast cup of rice
½ cup raisins or sultanas
6 cloves garlic
¼ teaspoon saffron *or*
  ¼ teaspoon turmeric

the juice of 2 lemons or limes
one inch cinnamon, crushed
salt to taste
¼ lb. blanched almonds
¼ cup Barbadoes sugar
2 dessertspoons butter

12 cloves
juice of 2 oranges
½ lb. carrots, grated
a pinch of aniseed—optional
4 five-oz. cartons of yogurt
20 peppercorns

1 pint milk
1 dessertspoon ground coriander
seeds from 12 cardamoms
4 large onions, finely sliced

Wash the duck thoroughly in salt water, then swill with fresh and prick all over with a fork. Work coriander, garlic, aniseed and a little salt into a paste an hour before operations begin. Melt a little butter, brown the onion in it, add carrot, raisins, sugar and orange juice, and when thoroughly amalgamated, add this to the paste already made, and stuff the duck with the mixture. Now mash the almonds into a pulp, add milk, lemon juice and the remainder of the butter and cook slowly into a thick sauce.

Place the duck in a tin in a medium-hot oven and baste with this sauce. When the duck is brown, place it in a deep casserole. Sprinkle the rice around it. Smear the duck with the remainder of the butter, strew it with cloves, cinnamon and cardamom seeds, put in enough water to cook the rice, and yogurt, saffron, peppercorns. Put on the cover of the casserole and cook for 5 minutes over high heat; then lower to just-simmering point and cook till rice is done. The water should have evaporated.

Enough for four.

FISH KOFTA WITH RICE

1 breakfast cup of rice
1 lb. filleted cod or haddock
3 egg yolks
1 tablespoon lemon or lime juice
6 oz. butter or ghee
¼ cup wholemeal flour
½ cup chopped parsley

1 teaspoon black pepper
½ cup mustard oil
½ teaspoon nutmeg
1 large onion, finely sliced
½ teaspoon ground cloves
1 wineglass of apple-cider vinegar, white wine or cooking sherry

Flake raw fish, mix with onion and fry in oil till golden brown. Do not put the fish in till the oil is well heated and a wisp of smoke rises from it. Fry till the fish is soft and a golden colour. Drain away oil and when the fish has cooled, mix it with egg yolk, nutmeg and parsley and mould it into balls with the help of flour.

Now melt the butter and at sizzling point sprinkle in the clove powder and fry for *10 seconds*. Add rice and stir over a medium heat for 7 minutes. Pour in cider or wine; cook for a minute longer, then add pepper, fish balls and lemon juice.

Pour in water slowly so that the rice is covered by at least an inch of water, bring to the boil, put on a tight-fitting lid and lower heat to simmering point. The rice should be tender by the time the water has evaporated; if not, add a little more. It is better to have too little than too much water, for water can always be added, and at simmering heat little damage can be done.

Apple cider vinegar imparts a tang that sherry or white wine does not—and is much cheaper. Try all three at different times.

Enough for four.

PRAWN PILAU

1 lb. shelled prawns	seeds from ½ doz. cardamoms
one inch of cinnamon	3 cloves of garlic
5 oz. bottle of cream	1 tablespoon lemon or lime
1 dessertspoon coriander	juice
powder	4 oz. butter
½ teaspoon black pepper	1 teaspoon turmeric
1 dessertspoon chopped mint	1 pint vegetable stock
2 breakfast cups rice	salt to taste
2 bay leaves	2 five-oz. cartons of yogurt

Boil the stock, add salt, pour over the prawns and cook till tender. Only very little cooking is needed. Then drain, but keep the stock. Put the prawns in a casserole or shallow pan, pour the butter, well heated, over them, and cook for five minutes. Add bay leaves, yogurt, coriander, garlic crushed, and stock; bring to the boil and remove from the stove. Cover with cream.

Cook the rice in a generous quantity of boiling water for not more than 10 minutes and drain away water. Place in a large pan, add the prawns, etc., and mix gently. Now sprinkle in cardamom seeds, cinnamon (crushed), pepper, mint and turmeric and mix with a fork.

Put the mixture back into the casserole, put on the cover and cook in an oven pre-heated to about 200°F. for 20 minutes. Test rice for softness and if done, remove and sprinkle with lemon juice and serve. If not done, cook till soft. If moisture is needed, add more stock or water.

It is always best to test the rice because cookers, voltages and gas pressures vary in different parts of the country, and at different times of the day.

Enough for four.

EGG PILAU

8 hard-boiled eggs	2 teaspoons cummin seed
2 cups Patna rice	1 tablespoon fennel seed
2 onions, finely sliced	9 cloves
2 tablespoons butter	6 cardamoms, shelled
1½-inch stick green ginger, mashed	1 inch cinnamon
6 cloves garlic, ground	2 teaspoons ground turmeric
2 green chillis, mashed	parsley

Fry onions till golden-brown in a fairly large saucepan, then put in two cups of water, the cloves, cardamom and cinnamon, mix, put on the lid and simmer for 10 minutes. Use a pan with a close-fitting lid. Add ginger, garlic, green chillis, cummin and fennel seed, mix, and place the rice on top. Add two cups of water, cover and simmer. Make a paste of the turmeric and a little boiling water, thin it down till liquid, and add to the contents of the pan. Cut the eggs into halves and place gently on the cooking rice.

Continue to simmer till the rice is soft, which should coincide with the evaporation of all the water, because any volume of rice, if simmered in a tightly closed pan with twice its volume of water, should be done by the time the water evaporates. In practice owing to many factors, this does not always work out, so it is best to test the rice from time to time.

Turn all carefully into a large open dish, garnish with parsley, and eat with poppadams (or pappadams), chutney or pickle, and if you like them, Bombay duck, either whole or crumbled.

Enough for four very generous helpings.

RICE KOFTAS

1 cup Patna rice	oil or fat, for frying
2½ cups milk	2 eggs
2 oz. butter	4 cloves garlic
½ teaspoon chilli powder	1 tablespoon chopped parsley

2 onions, minced	1 cup grated cheese
4 tablespoons canned tomato or tomato sauce	½ teaspoon ground cummin
	½ teaspoon ground turmeric
breadcrumbs	salt

Cook the rice in milk, till milk has evaporated, when rice should be tender. (More milk is needed than if water alone were used, as milk contains fat and protein solids.) If rice is not tender, add more milk. When tender, remove from stove. Mix with butter, salt, chilli powder, cummin and turmeric. Chop parsley finely, and together with onion, garlic, cheese and tomato, add to the rice mixture. Mix thoroughly. Shape into balls, roll in beaten egg and then in breadcrumbs, and fry till golden brown in deep, boiling fat. Remove and drain. Enough for 2, if served alone. But rice koftas go well with grilled or baked herrings, in which case they will make a meal for 4.

Try tomato sauce the first time, and canned tomato the next, to find out which you prefer. Only half a teaspoon of chilli powder is given, but if you like it hotter, add to this quantity next time. It is better to be conservative at first.

Enough for two or four.

KHICHIRI AND SAUCE

There are so many kinds of khichiri, and the ways in which they are made differ so vastly, that one often hears people say, 'Oh, but *that's* not khichiri!' It may not be one of the many kinds that they have tasted.

½ lb. Patna rice	½ teaspoon cummin seed
¼ lb. lentils	½ teaspoon turmeric
salt	¼ lb. butter, dripping or
1 large onion	other cooking fat or oil
1 pint water or stock	

Slice onion finely and fry till brown, then pour off half the fat into a small dish. Add turmeric and cummin seeds to the browned onions and fry for a couple of minutes. Turn the fried ingredients into a large pan, add rice and lentils, the remainder of fat, and mix well. Pour in the stock and salt. Put on close-fitting lid and simmer very gently till the rice is done. If there is still some water, pour it away. If the water has evaporated, and the rice still remains un-cooked, add a little *boiling* water.

If the instructions are carried out, the rice should be just cooked to a turn when the last drops of water evaporate.

The khichiri part is easy to make; now for the sauce.

Ingredients for Khichiri Sauce

2 cups of water or vegetable stock
1 pint fresh prawns or 1 lb. of any other fish
1 large onion
4 oz. butter, dripping or margarine
½ lb. tomatoes

a generous pinch of black pepper
2 eggs
4 tablespoons wine vinegar, or apple cider vinegar
6 cloves garlic
a generous handful of parsley
salt

Fry onions till golden brown, finely slice tomatoes and add, with parsley, garlic, pepper and salt. Fry till nearly dry. Pour on two cups of water or stock, bring to boil.

Clean prawns or fish (if fish, cut into pieces); put them in a saucepan, pour over the fried mixture and boil gently till soft.

Beat the eggs well, mix with vinegar and pour over prawns or fish just before serving.

The khichiri and the sauce must be served in separate dishes, and both should be piping hot.

Pappadams and sweet mango chutney go well with this dish; or a *saag* made with pounded green herbs, such as mint, to which a little sugar, vinegar etc., have been added.

If the sauce is too greasy, use less butter. Indians in the cities usually eat far more ghee or butter than Europeans, who sometimes find curries indigestible—and for no other reason.

Enough for four.

CHAPTER FOUR

More and Different Curries

CRAB KOFTAS

Koftas, of fish or meat minced or chopped very finely, mixed with
seasoning and moulded into balls, are invariably tastier than fish or
meat not so treated. And of all kofta curries, crab, lobster and
prawn are the most delectable.

1 lb. crab, lobster or prawn *meat*	8 oz. mustard oil or ghee
1 dessertspoon chopped parsley	4 red or 2 green chillis
	12 peppercorns
1 teaspoon chopped mint	1 breakfast cup tomato juice
1 teaspoon chopped tarragon	1 breakfast cup breadcrumbs
4 blades lemon grass	1 large egg, well beaten
6 bay leaves	1 teaspoon ground cummin
2 large onions, finely sliced	4 cloves garlic, chopped
1 dessertspoon coriander seeds	a pinch of ginger

Half-cook the meat and break it up; if need be, pound it. Chop
parsley, mint, tarragon and garlic finely and mix with the meat.
Then add ginger, peppercorns and coriander seeds and again mix. Wet
it with tomato juice (or water) and mould it into balls about 1½ inches
in diameter, dip in egg and roll in breadcrumbs. If the white of egg
is first beaten stiff and yolk then added, the crumb will hold better.

Heat the mustard oil or ghee, add chopped chillis, cummin and onions and fry till the onions are light brown. Put in the lemon grass and bay leaves, gently roll in the meat balls and simmer till done (about 10–15 minutes).

Remove lemon grass and bay leaves before serving. Crab Koftas are best eaten with plain rice and lemon, lime or bamboo pickle.

Vegetarian koftas, which are also tasty, can be made by using all these ingredients, but substituting Granose Nut Meat, or Vegarian Savoury Meal for crab.

Enough for four.

FISH KABAB

Kababs are traditional Muslim dishes and consist usually of beef, whole or minced, mutton, chicken, etc., and not fish. Fish Kabab is eaten, however, in Bengal, where fish and not flesh is the staple food of a riparian population.

pan of deep fat or
   mustard oil
1 lb. cod or haddock
2 large onions, minced
2–3 onions, sliced
1 teaspoon butter
2 inches green ginger
1 teaspoon cummin seed
1 tablespoon chopped parsley
12 peppercorns
½ teaspoon powdered cloves
½ teaspoon chilli powder
2 eggs
salt to taste
1 dessertspoon chopped
   marjoram

Boil fish till tender and set aside to cool. Heat a teaspoon of butter, toss in the onion and fry until golden. Chop parsley and marjoram very finely, and mix with ginger, cummin seed, peppercorns, cloves and chilli powder. Beat eggs well. Flake fish and mix with beaten egg, salt, spices and herbs. Form into two-inch balls.

Heat the fat till a wisp of smoke rises from the surface, then gently pop in the fish balls and cook till they are light brown. Remove, place on skewers with rounds of sliced onion between balls, and serve.

The fish balls may be rolled in breadcrumbs before cooking, but this is optional. Rolling in crumb gives a firm outside skin.

Enough for four.

STUFFED BRINJAL WITH BOMBAY DUCK

8 pieces of Bombay duck (a species of dried Indian fish)
4 medium-size brinjals (aubergines)
8 tablespoons fresh grated coconut, or desiccated coconut
4 large onions
8 cloves garlic
4 dessertspoons ground coriander
2 teaspoons ground turmeric
1 teaspoon ground cummin
1 teaspoon ground red chillis
8 tablespoons mustard oil or ghee for frying. Oil is best.
lemon juice

Slice onions finely and fry, together with the garlic, till the onions are golden brown. Add coriander, cummin, turmeric and red chillis and cook briskly for 5 minutes.

Boil brinjals till soft; then hollow them out and cut off the tops. Mix the curry ingredients with the brinjal pulp and simmer for three minutes. Add grated coconut, mix well and stuff the pulp back into the hollowed brinjals. It should fit, as cooking evaporates a good deal of the moisture. Replace the tops and bake in moderate oven for 15 minutes (no fat is required—bake dry).

Serve with lemon juice. Each brinjal should be served on a small mound of boiled rice, or with two chappattis, and two sticks of fried, crumbled Bombay duck. Bombay duck can be bought in packets and cooked under a grill, or fried with a little fat.

Those unaccustomed to it may find the odour of Bombay duck a trifle overpowering, but if this initial distaste can be overcome, they may even acquire a passion for it.

Enough for four.

CAMP FISH

The call of the outdoors is strong in Britain, even if the sun is not, and picnicking has a much stronger appeal to most of us than meals eaten sedately in the orthodox way. To fishermen there is no reward so great as a fresh trout, salmon—or even a coarse fish—whisked from a stream and cooked on a camp fire. What one needs is:

1 fish 9" or more in length	1½ teaspoons coriander
salt	½ teaspoon cummin
garlic—6 cloves	a handful of parsley
1 large onion	a sheet of tinfoil or
1 or two large tomatoes	a ball of string
1 teaspoon turmeric	

Open and clean the fish, using plenty of salt water. Chop onion, garlic, tomatoes and half the parsley and stuff inside the fish. Then close and lightly tie it. Rub fish all over (inside, too, if you wish, before stuffing) with paste made from coriander, cummin and turmeric.

Dig two holes, one on either side of the camp fire, and erect two stout stakes. Wait till the fire has died down and there are no flames. Then tie the fish, by head and tail, to the stakes, some distance above the still glowing embers; the distance above the fire to be regulated by the size of the fish. This will be gained by trial and error but in any case the fish will *ultimately* cook. Garnish with parsley.

An alternative method is to wrap the fish in tinfoil—double foil, if need be—and place it in the heart of the embers, under the dying fire. Continue fishing, and in an hour or so the fish will be ready—cooked in its own juices. All you then need is some bread with it.

DRY SHARK CURRY

1 lb. shark or cod	enough coconut oil for
2 tablespoons chilli powder	cooking
1 teaspoon saffron or turmeric	3 cloves garlic
1½ tablespoons mustard	3 slices green ginger
2 or 3 curry leaves	3 green chillis

| 1 tablespoon vinegar | 1 inch piece rampe |
| 2 large onions, sliced | 1 inch piece sera |

If new to curries, or if you've never tried this curry before, it would be advisable to start with 2 *teaspoons* of chilli powder and 1½ *teaspoons* of mustard, instead of *tablespoons*. You can always increase the quantities next time; and if you dislike cooking in coconut oil, as so many do, then use mustard oil, ghee or butter.

Wash and cut fish into slices, place in pan, cover with vinegar and a little water, and boil. When tender, remove fish. Mash ginger and garlic and mix with the chilli powder, turmeric (or saffron) and mustard, using a little water to form a paste. Smear this paste over the fish.

Heat a dessertspoon of oil or fat, fry the onions till golden brown, put in the rampe, sera and curry leaves, then fish and green chillis. Simmer the fish on one side, then turn and simmer again, altogether for 10 minutes. A little brown sugar may be sprinkled over the curry after it is taken from the stove. There is very little gravy in this curry; only if it tends to stick should you add a little water. Eat with rice and sweet mango chutney.

MRS YVETTE LOOS   *Enough for two.*
KINGSTON
NEGOMBO
CEYLON

CURRIED KIDNEYS

2 oz. butter or margarine	salt to taste
8 kidneys	1 teaspoon chilli powder
4 large tomatoes or 1 can	1½ teaspoons coriander
tomato pulp	1 teaspoon turmeric
4 onions, finely sliced	½ teaspoon cummin
1 can of garden peas	¼ teaspoon ginger
the juice of one lemon	

It is preferable to use one large can of tomato pulp for this dish instead of tomatoes, as tomato pulp is made from really sun-ripened tomatoes from Italy, Rumania or some country where tomatoes really do ripen in the sun.

Put the chilli, coriander, cummin, turmeric and ginger into a small bowl, add a little water and mix into a paste. Then add boiling water; keep mixing till the amount of water is about one breakfast cupful. Add the salt.

Slice the kidneys, which should already have been washed and cleaned.

Fry the onions in fat, till golden brown, add the curry spices; bring to the boil, put in the slices of kidney and turn each one.

Cover with the tomato pulp and continue cooking till the kidneys are soft. When that stage is reached, most of the tomato juice should have evaporated, leaving a thick gravy.

Put in the can of peas, shake till they are covered, cook for a minute and turn out into a dish.

Sprinkle with lemon juice and if you wish, garnish with parsley. Best eaten with chappattis or parattas and sweet mango chutney.

Enough for four.

DUCK RAICHATH

1 fat duck
2 tablespoons chopped onions
1 tablespoon chopped ginger
1 tablespoon green chillis
1 dessertspoon chopped garlic
salt

1 tablespoon Barbadoes sugar
1 coconut
1 tablespoon ground coriander
2 tablespoons vinegar

Wash, clean and cut duck into pieces. Grate coconut as finely as possible—if you can't buy a coconut, use desiccated coconut—and extract two lots of milk from it—a cupful each time. (See p. 9.)

Put pieces of duck into deep pan with the second extract of milk and a little water, and boil till tender. The water will evaporate and the fat from the duck will rise to the top. Pour this fat off, and fry the pieces of duck in it. If the duck is a good fat one, there will still be some fat in the frying pan or deep pan, whichever you use.

Remove the pieces of duck to a plate, and keep warm. Now add onions, ginger, chillis, garlic and coriander to the fat and fry them well for five minutes. Put in fried pieces of duck, sugar, vinegar and salt, cook for a further five minutes, or until the pieces are tender enough to be eaten, add the first extract of coconut milk, bring to the boil and remove from the stove.

Duck made in this way is extremely tasty without being too rich. If too pungent, use half the quantity of chillis. Serve with plain boiled rice, a lentil dish, and yogurt.

A satisfying meal for four.

CURRIED TRIPE

Tripe, that is, the first and second stomach of a ruminant, is not a traditional Indian dish, and most Indians, especially Hindus, will not touch offal. Here one suspects the hand of the Anglo-Indian, who makes the best of both worlds.

½ oz. of ghee, butter or mustard oil
1 large onion, finely sliced
1 oz. powdered coriander
1 teaspoon ground turmeric
1 teaspoon mustard (powder)
a generous pinch of black pepper

½ pint coconut milk *or*
¼ lb. desiccated coconut
1 lb. tripe
3 red chillis, seeded
6 peppercorns
4 large cloves garlic
1 inch green ginger
1 lime or lemon or tamarind

Cover the tripe with water, bring it to the boil and simmer till soft. Then drain off, but keep the liquor. Cut the tripe into 1½" pieces. Heat butter or oil, add onion and fry till light brown, then toss in ginger, mustard, turmeric and garlic, and brown. Now add the spices: coriander, black pepper, chillis and peppercorns. Simmer for a minute, put in the tripe, mix well and cover with the tripe water into which the desiccated coconut has been mixed. Stir gently and continue to simmer for five minutes. If coconut milk is used, do not keep the liquor from the tripe, but add coconut milk to the condiments.

Serve hot, with lime or lemon juice; or alternatively, with tamarind pulp mixed with a little water, and poured over the tripe. Tripe curry should be eaten with rice.

Enough for four.

BRAIN CURRY

The ancient belief that eating certain organs will give you some of the qualities those organs possess no longer holds good, but even so, brain curry is a favourite with many.

3 whole sheep's brains
2 large onions, sliced
1 large tomato, sliced
1 dessertspoon cummin seed
1 dessertspoon coriander seed
10 oz. yogurt
salt to taste

$\frac{1}{2}$–1 teaspoon chilli powder
the juice of one lemon
1 teaspoon turmeric
1 small sprig rosemary
a handful of parsley
4 oz. mustard oil or ghee

After cleaning and washing the brains in salt water, plunge them into boiling water, remove and place them in a dish for half an hour, then cover with cold water to which the lemon juice and rosemary have been added. Heat the water, and when it boils, remove the brains. Heat the fat or oil, add first the onion and then the tomato, and fry till the onion is brown. Put in the cummin, coriander, chilli, turmeric, salt, and cook for five minutes, then add yogurt and cook for another ten till the mixture thickens. Then add the brains, and if need be, a little water, and simmer for 5–10 minutes.

The addition of rosemary to the water gives an unusual tang which some find very pleasant. Before serving, sprinkle with chopped parsley.

Brain curry can be eaten with rice, chappattis or parattas, or on thick rounds of wholemeal bread, toasted.

Enough for four.

CHAPTER FIVE

More Vegetable and Fruit Curries

STUFFED BRINJALS

Brinjals or aubergines, the fruit of the Egg-plant *Solanum Esculentum*, may be prepared in many ways, some already described in the three previous curry books, but there are few tastier than stuffed brinjals.

4 large brinjals
4 green chillis, chopped
3 teacups of mixed vegetables —(carrots, potatoes, celery)
4 large cloves of garlic
1 tablespoon coriander powder
2 teaspoons powdered cummin
8 cloves
seeds from 8 cardamoms
2 oz. butter or ghee or mustard oil
salt to taste
½ teaspoon powdered ginger
1 large chopped onion

Dice and cook mixed vegetables until soft but firm. Cut the brinjals into halves, scoop out and simmer the middles in boiling water until soft. Fry onion in butter until golden, add chillis, garlic (mashed), coriander, cummin, cardamoms, cloves and ginger, and fry until brown. Mix the cooked spices, vegetables and scooped-out brinjal middles, add salt. Stuff brinjals with mixture.

If you have a steamer, place brinjals in it and steam until tender. If not, place in a casserole with a little butter and cook till tender. Serve with rice and some kind of acid pickle like lime or tamarind. Try both methods and see which you prefer.

Enough for four.

KHATTA CURRY

Khatta (khut/ta) is the Hindi word for acid, and khatta curry has a piquancy which may not, perhaps, appeal to all at first, but like ripe Roquefort cheese, grows on one.

¼ lb. carrots	1 tablespoon ground onion
¼ lb. potatoes	1 teaspoon turmeric
¼ lb. artichokes	½ teaspoon chilli powder
½ lb. pumpkins	4 cloves garlic, ground
1 lb. tomatoes, or a 1-lb. can of tomatoes	1½ teaspoons coriander
¼ lb. swedes	1 oz. tamarind
¼ lb. turnips	1 tablespoon *foot* sugar
1 teaspoon onion *seed*	4 green chillis
	2 or 3 oz. mustard oil

This dish is made in two stages.

1. Mix tamarind into a paste with a little water; then keep adding and mixing till a pint has been put in. Sweeten with the foot sugar and mix thoroughly. In India *jaggery* is used, but as this is not easily bought, foot sugar (black Barbadoes sugar) is the best substitute. Ask any big grocer for foot sugar and he will know what you mean. Strain the liquid into a jug.

2. Chop hard vegetables into inch or 1½ inch cubes and add tomatoes or canned tomato, just cover with water; toss in the ground onion, turmeric, chilli powder, garlic and coriander, bring to the boil, then simmer till half cooked.

Bring the mustard oil to such a heat that it gives off a wisp of smoke, then pop in the onion seed and fry for two or three minutes. Use a deep saucepan. Now pour in the tamarind water, add the half-cooked vegetables and bring to the boil. As soon as boiling point is reached, turn down the heat and simmer till the vegetables are cooked. Can be eaten cold or hot, with plain rice. No pickle or chutney is needed. Garnish with chopped green chillis.

Enough for four.

PUMPKIN CURRY

1½ lb. pumpkin
6 cloves garlic
1 inch of turmeric
2 red chillis
salt to taste
1 inch green ginger

2 green chillis
1 large onion
½ coconut
ghee or mustard oil for frying
     or butter or margarine

Cut pumpkin into inch or 1½-inch cubes. Grate coconut finely and mix well with one breakfast cup of cold water. Mash garlic, ginger and turmeric. Cut the red chillis into very fine pieces and add to this mash; then mix into the coconut water. Put the lot into a pan with the pumpkin and green chillis, which should be sliced lengthways, bring to the boil, then simmer till the pumpkin is tender.

Now fry the onion, which should also be sliced, and when brown, pour into pan. Stir, simmer for five minutes, season with salt and serve with plain white rice and crushed Bombay duck and pappadams; or alternatively, with lime pickle.

This is a very easily concocted dish. There is a tendency, however, to cook the pumpkin till it is too soft. If you do this, it becomes mushy and degenerates into a thick broth.

Enough for four.

BEAN FOOGATH

1 lb. French beans
1 large coconut
8 cloves garlic
4 green chillis
salt

8 small onions
1-inch piece green ginger
2 tablespoons butter or ghee
1 teaspoon powdered turmeric

Wash beans, strip the edges, slit and mince very finely. Place in a saucepan, with a small cupful of water, a shake of salt, 2 minced onions and the garlic. Boil till soft, simmer until all the water evaporates and remove from stove. Scrape coconut, mince remaining onions and chillis. In another saucepan, brown the onions in butter or ghee; then add the ginger, turmeric and chillis, finally the beans. Stir for three minutes and then remove. Now add the coconut, place on the stove again, stir for a minute or two and the foogath is ready. Eat with plain rice, or rice and lentils. Desiccated coconut may be used instead of a coconut: about 8–12 ounces.

Instead of beans, spinach or cabbage may be used. If so, substitute a teaspoon of black pepper for chillis. The use of turmeric is optional.

Enough for two.

MIXED VEGETABLE CURRY

The mixed vegetable curry one gets in the average Indian restaurant —even in the West End of London—is a travesty of the real thing: a potato or two, a carrot, a bean and a lady's finger (*okra*) swimming in a tepid greeny-brown ooze. Try this:

4 small brinjals	4 cloves garlic
4 potatoes	½ lb. carrots
4 large onions	1 can tomatoes (1 lb.)
½ lb. beans or green peas	6 red chillis
2 teaspoons coriander	1 teaspoon ground cummin
seeds of 3 cardamoms	1 inch turmeric
the flesh of one coconut	½ inch ginger
a small handful of coriander leaves	1 inch cinnamon
	1 teaspoon asafoetida
1 tablespoon butter or ghee	1 dessertspoon cooking oil

Halve, then soak, the brinjals with the potatoes and carrots in cold water. Mash the turmeric and ginger; break up cinnamon finely, and mix into a paste with the coriander, cardamoms, cummin, garlic and chillis, and fry spices with two sliced onions in a tablespoon of butter or ghee. Scrape the coconut and add. If you can't get a coconut, use ½ lb. desiccated coconut.

30

Put the cooking oil into a deep pan, bring to the boil and toss in the asafoetida. Now add the coconut mixed with curry spices, and the coriander leaves. Add ½ pint of water, bring to the boil, put in the brinjals, carrots, potatoes, tomato and peas (or beans), and two halved onions. Bring to the boil again, close with a well-fitting lid, and simmer till the carrots, beans etc. are soft. Most of the liquid should evaporate, leaving a thick, rich gravy.

Eat with plain rice and acid pickle.

Enough for four.

SIMPLE SPINACH CURRY

Spinach is not a vegetable that many try to curry, but if well curried, it makes an excellent supper dish. Incidentally, the top young leaves of ordinary stinging nettle—*urtica dioica*—can be treated in the same way, and taste like spinach, though a trifle stronger.

3 lb. spinach or young nettle leaves	a sprig of fennel
2 large onions, sliced, or 4 tablespoons minced spring onions or an equal quantity of shallots	a little—6–12 spikes—rosemary
	1 tablespoon butter, mustard oil or olive oil
6 cloves garlic, sliced lengthways	1 teaspoon cummin powder
6 green chillis, sliced lengthways	1 teaspoon coriander powder
	salt

Wash the spinach well. This is important as spinach is likely to gather grit. Take it out of the water and drop into a large, deep pan. Boil briskly without the addition of water, for about 8–10 minutes, by which time all the water clinging to the spinach will have evaporated and it will be cooked. Strain and squeeze dry. Cut the pulp into pieces. Fry the onions golden in oil or butter. The type of fat used will affect the flavour. Add garlic, chillis, cummin and coriander and fry for 3 minutes. Add this to the pan of spinach, together with fennel, rosemary and salt, cook for three minutes, then serve on toast or with chappattis and a little lime pickle.

The few drips of water squeezed from the spinach can be added during the final stages, and the spinach cooked till this becomes a thick gravy.

Enough for four.

DHALL BHATH

This is a typical Bengali (or Bengalee) dish; simple, easily made, and satisfying. It is also tasty if well made.

1 cup rice
1 cup lentils
3 green chillis
1 dessertspoon ghee or butter
   or mustard oil

4 cloves garlic
1 large sliced onion
1-inch stick of green ginger
1 teaspoon turmeric
salt

Boil the rice till soft, drain, and keep warm. Toss the lentils and salt into 1 pint of *boiling* water so that they break up quickly, and cook till fairly thick.

Brown the onion in fat, put in the chillis, garlic, ginger and turmeric, fry for 5 minutes, then mix with lentils and serve with rice, and pickle or chutney.

Enough for two.

FRUIT CURRY

2 large onions
1 small papaiya
1 slice pineapple
1 dessertspoon scraped coconut
1 tablespoon coconut cream
1 dessertspoon curry powder
1 cooking apple
1 dessertspoon butter

1 teaspoon milk
½ teaspoon ginger
1 teaspoon currants
2 bananas
½ lime or lemon
1 teaspoon sultanas
pepper or chilli powder
salt

Slice the onions finely and brown them in butter. Add curry powder, a teaspoon of milk, and cook briskly for five minutes. Cut the pineapple, papaiya, bananas and cooking apple into pieces, squeeze the lime or lemon over them, put in pan together with the onions and curry and cook for 10 minutes. Now turn the ingredients from the frying pan into a deep pan, add coconut cream, scraped coconut, ginger, currants, sultanas, pepper or chilli powder, salt, and simmer very gently for an hour and serve with boiled rice.

The papaiya is not common in England as yet, though it may be had from some of the bigger stores, such as Harrods, Fortnums, and Selfridges, when in season. The papaiya sold in Britain comes from the West Indies, where it is called a 'paw-paw'. The flesh is peachlike, and the middle filled with hundreds of small black seeds, like buckshot. These are easily scraped away with a spoon, and the green outside skin has to be discarded as well. It peels easily.

Serve with a border of boiled rice and pappadams.

Enough for four.

BREADFRUIT CURRY (Yam Curry)

It is possible at certain times of the year to get breadfruit, a product of the South Seas, which is farinaceous and has a whitish pulp the consistency of new bread, at some of the stores which sell exotic foods; and within the next decade, breadfruit should be as common as aubergines.

1 medium-size breadfruit	oil for frying
2 cups thick milk (coconut milk)	1 small onion, sliced
1 cup thin coconut milk	3 green chillis, sliced
2 cloves garlic	2 slices green ginger
1 tablespoon Bombay duck	1 sprig curry leaves
½ teaspoon saffron or turmeric	the juice of one lime or lemon
	salt

Clean and cut the breadfruit into round slices; then halve each slice and wash well. Put into a pan with a little oil and fry till golden. Add saffron (or turmeric) and lime (or lemon) juice and salt. Now add sliced onion, ginger, garlic, green chillis, powdered Bombay duck, curry leaves and the thin milk. Simmer. When the breadfruit is well cooked, add the 2 cups of thick coconut milk, stir well and remove from the stove.

This makes an excellent accompaniment to a beef curry. The thick coconut milk must be left till the dish is almost ready because coconut milk loses flavour if cooked too much.

Enough for four.

MRS YVETTE LOOS

PAPEETA CURRY

The *papeeta* (papaiya or paw-paw) already mentioned is a delicious fruit. In India it performs the same function as grapefruit in English homes and usually appears at breakfast. Lunches and dinners are often finished with *papeeta*, which has digestive properties. Here we eat melon. For those who are interested in such matters, *papeeta* contains 76% water (as much as the average potato), 5·2% protein, 0·9% fat, 16·8% carbohydrates, and 0·5% mineral matter. But, what no figures will convey, is its distinctive fragrant odour. Few Europeans realize that it can be concocted into curry; even fewer have tasted it in this guise. This is how it is made, and when, with the advance of quick-freezing, papaiyas flood our markets, you can try your hand. It won't be long.

1½ breakfast cups of papaiya cut into small cubes	4 small onions, sliced
3 rounded tablespoons grated or desiccated coconut	6 curry leaves
1 inch of turmeric	1 tablespoon of butter or cooking oil (butter much preferred)
2 or 3 green chillis (start with two)	salt optional (in my opinion unnecessary)
½ teaspoon cummin powder	

Put the papaiya pieces in a saucepan with 3 curry leaves and bring to the boil; then remove. Add salt, if you wish.

Mash turmeric, chillis and cummin, make into a paste with a little water, mix with grated coconut, add enough water to make a gravy, and simmer till thick. Add butter (or oil), onions and 3 curry leaves and bring to the boil; put in the curry-spice gravy, cook for a minute, pour over the papaiya and serve. To be eaten with plain rice.

Enough for two.

TOMATO CURRY

3 large tomatoes
1 teaspoon chilli powder
¼ dessertspoon fenugreek
1 dessertspoon sliced onions
1 dessertspoon dripping
1 or 2 cloves garlic

1 sprig curry leaves
1 dessertspoon Maldive fish
  or Bombay duck
1 breakfast cup coconut milk
one 1-inch piece cinnamon
salt

Select very large tomatoes; if you can't get very large ones, double the quantity. Cut them into thick slices—some like the pips removed. Sprinkle salt and chilli powder over them. Heat dripping in a small saucepan and add the fenugreek. Fry for five minutes. Put in garlic and fry for a further five minutes. Add sliced onions, cinnamon and curry leaves and fry till brown.

Slide in tomato slices and fry for another 15 minutes, stirring gently. Now add fish and coconut milk. Mix well, but try not to crush the tomato, and let the curry simmer gently till thick.

Tomato curry hasn't enough body to comprise the main dish of any meal; it is usually an adjunct in a dinner consisting of a number of dishes; or it can be eaten as a supper dish on a cold night. It is tasty and may be eaten with any type of rice, parattas, chappattis, or bread from a loaf.

Enough for four.

MRS DOROTHY THOMPSON
PANSALATENNE ESTATE
UKUWELA
CEYLON

CHAPTER SIX

Some Regional Variations

CURRIES VARY tremendously, and it would be quite wrong to assume that a mutton or chicken curry of one part of India will be cooked in much the same way in every other province (or in Ceylon or Malaya). There are other differences, too, in the cuisine.

In the North-West (now Pakistan) less rice is eaten than in other parts, much of it in the form of *pilau*. This is also true of Uttar Pradesh where *chappattis* (unleavened bread) and *dhall* are staple foods. Nor is fish highly regarded, though it may accompany the main dish. Milk, lentils, wholewheat bread and goat-mutton, with vegetables, comprise the meals of the North and North-West.

In Bombay, the most cosmopolitan city in India, the cuisine has infinite variety and some swear that the best food in India is to be had there.

But the Bengali will challenge that, for where can one eat fish and prawn curries like those made in the typical Bengali home: fish curries concocted with succulent bamboo shoots and the sweet, scented milk of young coconuts? Anglo-Indians will swear that their cookery comprises all that is best of East and West; but the Goanese bear the reputation of being the best cooks of all.

Whereas the food in Bombay, the North-West and the North is cooked in *ghee* (clarified butter), many Bengali dishes are prepared in mustard oil, and food in the South in coconut oil.

As one journeys South to Madras and then along the West coast, curries are prepared in ways peculiar to the region and flavoured differently. Here the accent is on pungency rather than on piquancy, and pepper-waters and chilli-curries make the newcomer—even those accustomed to curries all their lives—gasp and perspire.

CORNED-BEEF BHURTA

Corned-beef bhurta is, of course, an Anglo-Indian concoction, for corned-beef is a British or perhaps American invention. But it was

36

a staple food of the British Army and of civilians who existed in the *mofussil* far from the amenities of civilized life. They acquired a taste for curry but were suspicious of meat bought locally. In fact, in some parts of India it is difficult to get flesh in any form but fowl. And corned-beef bhurta is a compromise effected by the great race of improvisers.

1 tin corned-beef	1 lb. floury potatoes
2 onions	1 or 2 sprigs marjoram
3 green chillis	1 large sprig mint
the juice of 2 lemons	a little butter—optional

Chop the onions and chillis very finely. Pound the beef or work it with a fork till it is broken. Wash, dry and grate the lemons and add the grated peel to the beef. Squeeze the lemons. Then mix lemon juice, chillis and onions with the beef.

If the potatoes are new, don't skin, but scrub and boil them, and mash—if you wish, with a little butter and chopped mint and marjoram. Place the mashed potato in a dish and pile the corned-beef on top of it.

This is best eaten on rounds of hot buttered toast with ripe tomatoes.

Enough for four.

PINEAPPLE-BEEF

Pineapple-beef is another Anglo-Indian dish, for beef is not usually eaten where pineapples flourish, and it needs imagination to combine the two. The dish, it is believed, was invented by Count Benoît La Borgne, better known as General De Boigne, who was born at Chambéry, in Savoy, and was one of the famous military adventurers of Hindustan.

1 lb. beef from the undercut of the sirloin	black pepper or chilli powder
	2 oz. butter
1 tablespoon Worcester or similar sauce	1 *ripe* pineapple (press to ensure it is soft)
salad oil—1 tablespoon	6 cloves of garlic
salt	

Cut beef into rounds the size of pineapple slices, and trim off all fat and skin. Place on a flat dish, rub well with sliced garlic, sprinkle with salt and pepper (or chilli powder) and douse first with sauce, then with oil. Stand for four hours.

Now peel the pineapple, cut it into rounds, and fry lightly in the butter. Grill the rounds of beef. Put them on a large flat dish on

37

a hot plate and place one pineapple slice on each round of grilled beef. Serve on fried bread.

Enough for four.

SAVOURY BEEF (Ceylon)

2 lb. beef from rump or round
3 large onions, sliced
3 tablespoons fat or oil
½ teaspoon pepper
1 tablespoon ketchup
½ teaspoon powdered cummin
6 bay leaves
salt to taste

1 pint vegetable or meat stock or boiling water or meat extract
3 tablespoons flour
3 tablespoons vinegar
4 cloves garlic
½ teaspoon powdered turmeric

Slowly brown the onions in fat or oil, then increase the heat.

Cut the beef into cubes and rub into them salt, pepper and vinegar.

Put the seasoned meat into the fat and onions. Fry.

Add the remainder of the spices: cummin, turmeric, garlic, bay leaves.

Make a paste with the flour and some more vinegar, and thin gradually with the stock, meat extract or plain boiling water. Add this to the meat, spices, etc., bring to the boil and then simmer till the meat is soft.

Add a tablespoon of ketch, cook for a minute more, serve hot.

While cooking this curry, almost all the liquid should evaporate, so it is necessary to stir a good deal. If need be, a little water should be added to prevent sticking, but not enough to make a gravy. It should be a dry curry.

To be eaten with rice and mango chutney or brinjal pickle, or with yogurt.

Enough for six.

MRS YVETTE LOOS

HOT MEAT CURRY (Ceylon)

1 lb. beef or mutton cut into ¾" cubes
1 oz. pickling onions, sliced
2 green chillis
½" piece of ginger, sliced
1 piece of rampe leaf
a few curry leaves
a few blades of lemon grass

1 oz. cummin paste
3 oz. ground pepper
3 oz. billin, sliced (a small, acid fruit), or lime or lemon
¼ teaspoon saffron or turmeric
1 oz. mustard or cooking oil
1 stick of celery

the milk of half a coconut, or milk made from ½ lb. of desiccated coconut and boiling water

1 oz. coriander paste
2 cloves garlic, sliced
¼–½ teaspoon powdered nutmeg, cloves and cardamom

Place the oil in a saucepan and heat it.

Mix the onion and chillis, coriander and cummin paste, pepper, billin, saffron (or turmeric), ginger, garlic, rampe, curry leaves, lemon grass and celery, and put them into the heated oil with the meat. Just cover with water, bring to the boil, and cook for half an hour. Stir from time to time to keep the ingredients from sticking or burning.

When the meat is tender, almost all the water should have evaporated, so pour over it the coconut milk. Simmer for two or three minutes, then remove from the stove and place in a heated dish.

Hot meat curry made this way should be eaten with plain boiled rice; and over the whole concoction should be sprinkled from ½ to ¼ teaspoon of roasted and powdered nutmeg, cloves and cardamom, which give it a delightful aroma and improve the taste.

The best pickle to accompany this curry is either lime or bamboo made from young shoots. Or eat with yogurt.

Enough for four.

MRS YVETTE LOOS

SHEIKH MAHSHI

This is a dish that has come by way of Iraq to India, and can be made either with aubergines, marrows or small pumpkins.

4 aubergines (brinjals)
½ lb. cold meat from previous meal
1 cup boiled rice
1 large onion
1 large tomato or ½ tin tomatoes
salt optional

butter for cooking—4 oz.
4 cloves garlic
4 sprigs parsley
1 teaspoon cummin
1 teaspoon turmeric
2 lemons

Remove the top and stem from each aubergine, and peel lengthways in alternate strips; that is, peel one strip and leave some skin; then peel another strip, and so on.

Remove as much of the inside of the vegetable as you can without weakening the shell. Perforate with a fork or pointed knife and soak in salt water for 15 minutes, then fry gently in butter till a golden brown.

Fry the cold meat, garlic, cummin and turmeric briskly for two minutes in 1 oz. of butter; then mix with the following ingredients finely chopped: onion, tomato, and parsley. Add the boiled rice and mix again. Stuff this mixture into the aubergines, replacing the end pieces.

Put the remainder of the butter into a large pan, heat; add the stuffed aubergines with a little water, salt if you wish, and the juice from two lemons. The lemons may be grated before being squeezed, and the grated skin added to the pulped mixture used for stuffing.

Cook till the aubergines are soft enough to eat. Don't boil briskly; simmer. Melons may be similarly treated if stuffed with a sweet mixture: raisins, sultanas, currants, dried bananas, etc.

Enough for four.

MALAY CUCUMBER CURRY

Though Indian influence may be seen in some Malay curries, these usually have a more delicate flavour and generally eschew coriander and cummin, which tend to overpower the flavour and perfume of coconut milk.

2 pints of shelled prawns
6 cucumbers or ¼ of a pumpkin
2 oz. ghee or butter
1 tablespoon ground onion
2 teaspoons turmeric powder
1 teaspoon chilli powder
4 small sticks (½″) cinnamon

2 blades lemon grass
½ teaspoon ground ginger
4 cloves mashed garlic
2 breakfast cups coconut milk
6 cloves
seeds of 6 cardamoms
salt to taste

Cut the cucumbers into 15–20 pieces. If pumpkin is used, remove the outer skin, cut it into 16 pieces each about two inches square, and steep in water for an hour. Fry all spices, except lemon grass, with onion in butter for 10 minutes on a medium heat, then add prawns and cook till soft. Put in cucumber pieces (or pumpkin) with water drained off, pour over this the coconut milk, add lemon grass, salt, and simmer gently for 30 minutes.

Before serving, remove the lemon grass.

Malay Cucumber (or Pumpkin) Curry is always eaten with rice, usually to the accompaniment of some acid pickle, like lime.

The quantity of chilli can be increased or decreased according to the sensitivity of your palate. I have been told by some who have been kind enough to use my books that my curries are not *hot* enough, but this can easily be remedied.

Enough for four.

STUFFED SNAKE-GOURD CURRY

Snake gourds have not, as far as I am aware, appeared on the stalls in our market places in any quantity, but small round, or cylindrical pumpkins will do.

1 snake gourd or pumpkin   ghee or butter for frying
milk from ½ a coconut

Stuffing ingredients

4 oz. onions, finely sliced   ½ lb. minced beef or beef left
2 teaspoons chilli powder   over from a previous meal
½ lb. boiled potatoes, diced   1 stick celery, chopped
4 oz. tomato pulp   ½ teaspoon fenugreek
1 green chilli, sliced   1-inch piece of rampe
3 curry leaves

A cylindrical pumpkin is best. Peel and wash it, then cut into pieces 2–3 inches thick, scoop out the centres, scald in salt water and drain.

Fry onions till light brown. Add beef and $\frac{1}{2}$ teaspoon of chilli powder and fry for a few minutes. Scrape flesh from coconut, pour $\frac{1}{2}$ pint of boiling water over it, allow it to stand for 10 minutes, then squeeze through muslin. This is the *first* milk. Repeat the operation. This is the *second* milk. Put both aside.

Thoroughly mix remainder of stuffing ingredients, add fried beef, and fill this mixture into the scooped-out pieces of pumpkin or snake gourd.

Put the pumpkin pieces in a deep wide pan, add the second milk and boil. As soon as boiling point is reached, simmer till the pumpkin is soft enough to be eaten. Then bring to the boil again, add the first milk and remove the pan from the flame. Shake the pan occasionally in cooking; don't stir, or the stuffed pieces will break.

Enough for four.

MRS NOELLE DENTROM
47/1 1ST CROSS STREET
PAGODA
NUGEGODA
CEYLON

CHICKEN WHITE CURRY

1 chicken
2 sprigs fennel
2 slices green ginger, chopped
10 red chillis, ground
$\frac{1}{2}$ teaspoon sweet cummin powder
$\frac{1}{4}$ teaspoon fenugreek
1-inch piece cinnamon
$\frac{1}{4}$ stem lemon grass
juice of $\frac{1}{2}$ lime or lemon
salt

1 dessertspoon sliced onion
2 cloves garlic
$\frac{1}{2}$ teaspoon saffron or turmeric
1 dessertspoon coriander seed
1 teaspoon white cummin seed
1 dessertspoon ghee
2-inch piece rampe
small sprig curry leaves
$\frac{1}{2}$ pint thick coconut milk
$1\frac{1}{2}$ pints second extract coconut milk

Dismember chicken and place pieces into a saucepan with the $1\frac{1}{2}$ pints—second extract—of coconut milk, fennel, garlic, ginger, saffron (or turmeric), red chillis, fenugreek, cinnamon, and half each of the onion, rampe, lemon grass and curry leaves.

Cook until chicken is parboiled, then make a paste of one dessertspoon of the thick coconut milk, coriander and cummin. Put in the remainder of the thick milk, stir, add lime (or lemon) juice and salt, and pour into saucepan. Simmer till chicken is tender.

Now heat the ghee, put in remaining ingredients and fry them; then turn into pan with chicken. Simmer for two or three minutes and serve with either plain rice or pilau.

Usually accompanied by lime or bamboo pickle, or some kind of bhurta.

Enough for four.

MRS YVETTE LOOS

LIVER CURRY

1 lb. liver	2 cloves chopped garlic
1 dessertspoon chilli powder	a 2-inch piece of cinnamon
1 dessertspoon curry powder	a small sprig of bay leaves
1 teaspoon saffron or turmeric	1 teacup thin coconut milk
1 clove garlic, chopped	$\frac{1}{2}$ teacup thick coconut milk
1 clove garlic, crushed	juice of one lemon
1 slice green ginger	1 dessertspoon dripping
$\frac{1}{2}$ teaspoon fenugreek	2 onions finely sliced
a 2-inch piece of screwpine	table-salt

Wash and cut liver into slices or cubes, then season with table-salt, curry powder and chilli powder, and set them aside for 15 minutes. Heat the dripping in a saucepan and put in the fenugreek. Stir for five minutes. Add crushed garlic and fry till it turns pale yellow. Follow with sliced onions, bay leaves, screwpine, cinnamon, chopped garlic and ginger, and fry till the ingredients are dark brown.

Put the liver into this concoction and fry for 15 minutes, stirring constantly to prevent the curry from sticking to the pan. Then add thin coconut milk, cloves and turmeric; stir thoroughly, cover pan and simmer gently till the liver is tender. Finally, add thick coconut milk and lemon juice and continue to simmer gently till the gravy is thick. *Do not cover the pan after the thick milk has been added.*

If eaten with plain white rice—Patna or Kashmiri—the full flavour is brought out; add a *sambal* or *bhurta* but no pickle or chutney.

Enough for four.

MRS DOROTHY THOMPSON

RABBIT CURRY

The British rabbit—rarer alas, than before the war—makes a tastier curry than chicken, especially broiler chickens mass-produced in factories, which are just about as tasteless as blotting paper.

1 large rabbit
½ oz. coriander seed
¼ oz. white cummin seed
⅛ oz. sweet cummin seed
½ teaspoon fenugreek
a 2-inch piece of screw pine
1 dessertspoon vinegar
the milk of one coconut
1 tablespoon sliced onion
a teaspoon of turmeric

6 cloves
1 clove garlic, sliced
2 slices green ginger, 1 inch each
a 2-inch piece of cinnamon
a small sprig of bay or curry leaves
1 tablespoon dripping
20 dry chillis—use less if a mild curry is wanted

Roast chillis, coriander and cummin seed till they are almost black, then grind them into a smooth paste. Cut the rabbit into neat joints, and place in a saucepan with sufficient coconut milk to cover. Add all the other ingredients except dripping and one teaspoonful of sliced onion. Mix thoroughly and let the curry boil gently till the rabbit is tender and the gravy fairly thick.

Heat the dripping in another saucepan and fry the remainder of the onion till it is golden brown. Add the pieces of rabbit and fry for about 15 minutes; then pour in the gravy and cook for a further five minutes, stirring the whole time.

Eat with white or yellow rice and pickle.

Enough for five.

MRS DOROTHY THOMPSON

BHOONA GOAST

Bhoona goasts are great favourites among Europeans and Anglo-Indians, and Pakistanis in particular excel in making them. There are many varieties of *bhoona goasts*, and they are usually eaten by Europeans and Anglo-Indians with *khichiri* (kedgeree); by South Indians with pepper water or *mooligatanee* (mulligatawny).

1 lb. mutton cut into cubes
1 tablespoon ghee or other fat

1 dessertspoon vinegar
4 cloves garlic, sliced

1 tablespoon finely minced onion	3 pickled chillis, sliced
1 tablespoon desiccated coconut	1 tablespoon curry powder
	salt to taste

Fry onion to a golden brown in ghee or other fat, add garlic and chillis, cook gently for a minute and stir in curry powder. Mix well and simmer gently for 5 minutes. Add meat and vinegar. Stir well, bring to the boil, then lower heat and simmer, stirring occasionally to prevent ingredients sticking to pan. When the meat is tender, add the coconut and stir briskly. Coconut absorbs moisture.

Bhoona goast is a dry curry with little or no gravy. If too dry and any of the contents tend to stick to pan, add a *little* water.

Remove from the stove the moment the meat is tender and eat *hot*, with chappattis, parattas or poorees.

Beef, pork and rabbit can also be cooked in the same way; so may leftover cold meats.

Enough for four.

MOLEE CURRY (South Indian)

8 small fish, such as herrings	2 teaspoons ground turmeric
½ coconut	1 tablespoon ground coriander
10 green chillis	
2 tablespoons sliced onions	1 teaspoon ground cummin
6 pickling onions	4 cloves garlic
1 tablespoon butter or cooking fat	3 red chillis
	6 curry leaves
1 tablespoon vinegar	1 teaspoon salt

Grate coconut finely and extract milk, about half a pint. If there is any natural coconut milk, reserve that. Clean fish and smear inside and out with paste made from ground turmeric, salt and a little warm water. Heat fat to boiling point, fry fish, and when done, place fish on flat dish on a hotplate. Throw sliced onions and curry leaves into the fat, and brown them; add coriander, cummin, garlic and dried chillis. Cook for 5 minutes. If too little fat is left over after cooking the fish, add a teaspoonful.

Put in coconut milk, pickling onions and green chillis sliced length-wise, then raise the heat till milk boils, and put in the vinegar. As the mixture thickens, put in the natural milk of the coconut; if there is none, add a little water. The gravy should be ready when there is no sign of oil on top.

Pour over fish and serve.

The ten green chillis make Molee Curry very pungent, so eat plenty of plain rice with it, and accompany it with bhurta or saag; not pickle or chutney.

Enough for four.

COCONUT PRAWN CURRY (South Indian)

½ a coconut
1 pint cleaned prawns
8 green chillis
½ teaspoon ground cummin
4 cloves garlic
4 small chopped onions

1 tablespoon oil or fat
tamarind—about the size of two marbles
6 curry leaves
salt

The prawns, when shelled and cleaned, should amount to about one pint.

Grind the coconut very finely (desiccated coconut will do), chop curry leaves into small pieces, and mix with coconut, chillis, cummin, onions and garlic into a paste with oil or fat. Mix the tamarind in water and strain to remove stringy pieces. Add tamarind water to the paste and increase the mixture to one pint, with warm water. Pour the mixture into a pan, and add prawns and salt. Cook and stir gently till the prawns are soft.

Serve with plain rice.

Enough for two.

DHOPA (South Indian)

A slice of fish weighing about 1 lb.
6 green chillis—sliced
1 tablespoon small onions—sliced—or one large onion, sliced
½ teaspoon black pepper

2 eggs
2 tablespoons vinegar
½ coconut—or 1 packet desiccated coconut
1½ teaspoons turmeric
salt

Clean and wash the fish, then rub it, inside and out, with a paste made of turmeric, salt and water, then steam or boil it in water till tender and put in a dish on a hotplate.

Grate coconut finely and extract the milk. If desiccated coconut is used, extract the milk with hot water. (See page 9.) Beat eggs and add sliced chillis, onions and pepper. Heat the mixture and when it comes to the boil, pour in the coconut milk. Stir, and as it thickens, add vinegar. Keep stirring and cooking till it thickens once more. Remove from stove, add salt, stir well and pour over fish.

This is a somewhat pungent concoction, as are most South Indian curries, and should be approached with circumspection, as a little goes a long way. It is, however, very agreeable with plenty of plain boiled rice. Dhopa is usually followed by a slice of melon, a fruit which assuages the internal fires.

Enough for two.

FRIED EELS

Fried eels are a favourite dish along the East coast of India.

2 eels	16 curry leaves
1 inch piece of turmeric	1 teacup mustard oil
6–8 garlic cloves	4 red chillis
a piece of tamarind the size of a marble	1 teaspoon cummin
salt	4 oz. butter

Clean and cut eels into rounds. Grind turmeric, garlic, chillis, cummin, salt and 12 curry leaves into a paste, and rub this well into the eel slices. Heat oil in a deep frying pan. Put in the tamarind and 4 curry leaves. Boil till the tamarind is very dark brown, then remove it and the curry leaves and discard them. The oil has now absorbed the flavour of the tamarind and the leaves and is 'seasoned'. Put the butter into the pan of oil and when boiling, slide in the slices of eel and fry golden brown or perhaps a trifle darker.

Serve with plain rice plentifully garnished with parsley.

Prawns and sea fish may be cooked in the same way and are extremely tasty, but the fisherman's favourite is fried eels.

Enough for six.

CHAPTER SEVEN

Soups, Savouries, Pickle Curries and Relishes

INDIAN CORN SOUP

'Indian' corn is a cereal not indigenous to India. It was taken there from America, for originally it came from Mexico. The real name is *maize*: Spanish *maiz*; Cuban *mahiz*, and in South American countries the maize-starch or flour used for food is known as *maizena*.

Maize or *bhootta*, as it is known in India, is a popular food, and the climate and soil suit it, for it is a deep-rooting plant that does not need much manure.

1 breakfast cup lentils	2 onions, finely sliced
3 pints water	1 tin Mexican sweet corn
1 teaspoon turmeric	1 teaspoon cummin powder
2 tablespoons finely chopped parsley	2 cloves garlic
	salt—very necessary

Mix the cummin and turmeric well in a couple of tablespoons of boiling water. Bring the 3 pints to the boil and pour in the lentils. Unless the water is boiling the lentils will not break up easily. Some soak lentils overnight in bicarbonate of soda to achieve this result, but this is harmful and usually causes heart-burn. Putting lentils into *boiling* water always breaks them up.

Now add turmeric, cummin, onions and garlic—and salt. Without salt, lentils are tasteless. Boil fairly hard for 10 minutes, then whisk till lentils are dissolved, and add the tin of sweet corn.

Ladle out in generous quantities in *bowls* and top with chopped parsley. This is a meal in itself, if eaten with brown bread or Ryvita or rye bread.

Enough for two.

MULLIGATAWNY SOUP

In the *Second Book of Curries*, one recipe for Mulligatawny Soup is given, but of course, there are many kinds; the liquor may be meat stock, the stock from pigs' trotters or the shin bones of sheep, or even water in which fish has been cooked. This recipe is for *one kind of Mulligatawny*.

A quart of vegetable stock *or* a quart of beef or other meat stock
4 oz. butter or ghee
1 large chicken
2 large onions, finely sliced
1 teaspoon powdered turmeric
½ teaspoon ground chillis—or more, according to taste
½ teaspoon ground or powdered ginger
1 teaspoon mashed garlic
½ teaspoon coriander powder
½ teaspoon cummin seed
2 oz. ground poppyseed
6 kurreah fool leaves
2 or 3 lemons, sliced
salt

Clean and cut the chicken into 15–20 pieces. Fry one of the sliced onions in little ghee or butter to a golden brown, and set it aside. Put the remainder of the butter or ghee into a deep, capacious pan, bring to sizzling point and add the second onion, ground into a pulp, the turmeric, chillis, ginger, garlic, coriander and cummin. As the mixture fries, add a tablespoon of water. After five minutes of stirring, put in the chicken and when the chicken is golden brown, add poppyseed, salt and stock, fried onion and *kurreah fool* leaves.

Place a close-fitting cover on the pot and simmer till the chicken is tender. Serve piping hot, and just before eating, squeeze lemon juice over the soup.

This soup may also be poured over rice that has been left over from a previous meal.

Enough for six.

PUMPKIN SOUP

Very few people in Britain ever think of pumpkins in terms of soup, yet a delicious soup can be made with either pumpkins or marrows.

In India it is also made with the squash, a vegetable of a similar species.

1 lb. pumpkin or marrow	4 cloves garlic
3 oz. butter or ghee	1 teaspoon turmeric
4 small onions, finely sliced	$\frac{1}{2}$ teaspoon cummin
6 cloves	$\frac{1}{2}$ teaspoon chilli powder
12 peppercorns	or 2 green chillis
1 tablespoon Worcester sauce	salt
or 1 tablespoon vinegar	handful of parsley
2 pints vegetable stock	2 eggs

Skin the marrow or pumpkin and remove the seeds, though some like the seeds. Slice or cut it into cubes. Wash and drain. Heat butter in a deep saucepan and fry the vegetable briskly for 5 minutes. Then add onions, turmeric, cummin and chilli powder and fry again for 5 minutes.

Now pour the vegetable stock over it, put in the cloves, garlic and peppercorns, bring to the boil and then simmer till the pumpkin (or marrow) is very soft and pulpy. Strain this into a large basin and add sauce (or vinegar) and salt.

While all this is being done, boil the eggs till hard; shell and halve them. Mince the yolk and cut the whites into strips. When the soup is strained and ready, add the eggs and serve, well garnished with parsley. Always use either butter or ghee, never margarine or other fat, for butter makes all the difference to the taste.

Enough for four.

CURRIED POTATOES

12 potatoes	$1\frac{1}{2}$ teaspoons turmeric
8 dry (red) chillis	1 teaspoon coriander
2 eggs	4 ounces butter or ghee
salt	

Scrub, then boil potatoes in their jackets till soft but firm. Remove and peel, cut in halves. Beat eggs well. Grind or chop chillis very finely, mix with egg, a little salt. Mix the turmeric and coriander into a thick, smooth paste, thin with a tablespoon of boiling water, add egg mixture and beat rapidly till thick.

Boil the fat in a frying pan, dip the potato halves into the egg mixture and fry till brown. Remove, drain and serve either with parattas or chappattis, or with cold meat. A tasty savoury for supper on a cold winter's night.

Enough for four.

POTATO BADUN

½ lb. potatoes
½ teaspoon saffron or turmeric
1 dessertspoon chilli powder
2-inch piece of rampe
4 onions, finely sliced
a breakfast cup of thick
   coconut milk
3 tablespoons cooking oil

1 dessertspoon Maldive fish
   or 1 dessertspoon Bombay
   Duck
a sprig of curry leaves
1-inch slice of ginger
3 cloves garlic, chopped
salt

Boil and then peel the potatoes. Cut into thick slices, put into a saucepan and cover with coconut milk. Add remainder of ingredients, except the onions and oil, and cook till the potatoes are soft enough to eat, but firm. Then fry the onions in the oil in another pan, and when golden-brown, empty in the contents of the first pan. Continue to simmer till the liquid evaporates and the gravy is almost non-existent.

Eat with bread, chappattis, or plain rice and a little lime pickle.

A tit-bit for two.

MRS YVETTE LOOS

KALUPOL SAMBOL

½ coconut or ½ lb.
   desiccated coconut
3 onions
12 red chillis
juice of 1 lime or lemon

1 tablespoon Maldive fish or
   1 tablespoon Bombay duck
1 teaspoonful fat or oil
salt

Scrape the flesh from half a coconut, or use desiccated coconut, put it in a pan and roast over a low heat till light brown. Then turn out on to a flat dish. Peel and slice onions finely, and roast them, too, in a little fat or oil. Put into the dish with the coconut. Roast the fish (or Bombay duck) and the red chillis, and put them into the dish as well. Each item must be roasted separately.

Place all the ingredients on a *seel* or grinding stone and grind well. Then add salt, lime juice, mix and mould into a ball. Serve.

To be eaten with curry and rice.

MRS YVETTE LOOS

BRAIN CUTLETS

4 sheep's brains
1 dessertspoon parsley

1 teaspoon chilli powder
a pan of deep fat

1 dessertspoon thyme	1 large egg
1 large onion	wholemeal breadcrumbs
6 cloves garlic	1 floury potato
a little butter	

Wash brains, then plunge into boiling water. Remove and plunge into cold water and bring to boil. Remove and allow to cool. Boil and mash the potato with a little butter, and mix in chilli powder. Whisk egg till stiff. This is best done by first whisking the white, then adding the yolk.

Chop brains, parsley, thyme, onion and garlic and mix all, with potato, thoroughly. Mould this mixture into cutlets and dip in the beaten egg; then roll in breadcrumbs. Fry in deep fat till light brown, remove and drain.

There are many variations of stuffing that can be used in making brain cutlets: tarragon, rosemary, marjoram, thyme, etc. Experiment with them, though *if rosemary is used, put in very little* as this herb is pungent and too much can spoil the dish.

Brain cutlets should be eaten with *chappattis* and one of many kinds of *bhurta*. Rice and brain cutlets do not make the best combination.

Enough for four.

CHINGREE PUFFS

Chingree puffs or patties are a favourite with Anglo-Indians—especially for tea or picnics. 'Tea' in such establishments is really a high tea, in which left-overs from 'tiffin' (lunch) appear, as well as cheese, guava cheese, palm fruit in hot weather, and other delicacies to titillate the jaded palate.

¾ lb. self-raising flour	½ pint shelled prawns
10 oz. ghee or butter	1 teaspoon ground coriander
2 oz. sliced onions	1 teaspoon ground turmeric
¼ teaspoon salt	½ teaspoon ground cummin

Mince or pound prawns into a paste, having *first* removed heads, tails and shells. Heat 2 oz. of fat and fry the sliced onions till brown. Mix the coriander, turmeric and cummin with a little water, into a paste, add a cupful of *boiling* water, and stir. Pour over onions and keep stirring for 3 minutes on a medium heat. Add prawns and salt, and cook gently for 5 minutes.

Use 4 oz. of the fat with the flour to make either short or puff pastry. Roll it out very thin, cut into rounds or squares, fill the middles generously with curried prawns and fold over, as if making jam puffs. Close the edges carefully.

Put the remaining fat into a large frying pan, bring to the boil, slide in the puffs and fry till they are light brown in colour. Remove and drain. The puffs should be very light and tasty.

Alternately, they can be put into a hot oven and cooked like pastry. Meat can be used instead of prawns, but is nothing like as tasty.

Enough for at least twelve puffs.

OMELETTE CURRY

The omelette is not an Indian dish, but curried omelettes—and there are innumerable varieties—are an excellent compromise between East and West. There are few tastier dishes.

Note: To make omelettes well, very little fat is needed, but it is essential to have a thick, special omelette pan. (An excellent one can be bought from Madame Cadec, 27 Greek Street, London W.I.) A thick pan retains the heat, so that the heat can be turned off once the pan is hot, and there will be no fear of burning.

6 eggs	2 cloves garlic
2 onions—finely sliced	½ teaspoon turmeric powder
2 green chillis—minced	½ teaspoon coriander powder
½ lb. of any cold meat left over: mutton, liver, bacon, beef, or even parts of chicken, grouse, etc.	¼ teaspoon cummin powder
	a pinch of ginger
	2 oz. butter
	salt

Place 1 oz. butter in a frying pan and heat. Brown the onions in it, then add turmeric, coriander, cummin, chillis, garlic and ginger and cook for 5 minutes, stirring briskly. If too dry, add a little water.

Add the minced cold meat and cook for two or three minutes, till the meat is saturated. Add salt now, or after omelette is made.

Break the eggs into a bowl and mix till white and yolks are one—but not till stiff. Heat omelette pan well, melt butter, then pour in the eggs. Turn off the heat. Put the curried meat into the middle of the egg from north to south, or east to west, and when the egg starts to thicken and consolidate, use a flexible slice, and fold. Turn and heat for a few moments on the other side. Serve hot. Garnish with parsley and eat on hot toast.

Enough for four.

Bhajees

Bhajees are vegetable curries that are fried, for *bhajee* means *fried*, and the two most popular bhajees in India are probably made from *brinjals* (aubergines) and *pulwals*. Aubergines can be bought almost anywhere in England during the summer, for they are imported in large quantities from France; but the *pulwal*, a large, beanlike vegetable, is indigenous to the tropics.

BRINJAL BHAJEE

There are many kinds of brinjal bhajee, and this is perhaps the simplest of all, and the easiest if you have never tried this delicious vegetable. When selecting brinjals, don't pick the biggest, as big vegetables are usually old and have the toughest skins.

2 medium-size brinjals weighing ½ lb. each	1 teaspoon powdered turmeric
1 breakfast cup of mustard oil or butter	½ teaspoon chilli powder
	salt to taste

Wash the brinjals thoroughly and slice them into rounds no more than an eighth of an inch thick. If much thicker they will not cook easily and quickly. Do *not* skin them. Steep them in cold water for an hour, then remove and dry them. Mix the turmeric, salt and chilli into a paste with water, and apply this to both sides of each slice of brinjal.

Pour the mustard oil into a large frying pan and heat it till blue smoke issues; then pop in as many slices of brinjal as the pan will hold and fry till golden brown. Prod with a fork or sharp pointed knife to test whether they are tender. Fry on both sides.

When the slices are done, place them in a warm dish and eat with plain boiled rice accompanied by lime pickle; or with *poorees*, or rolled up in *chappattis*.

If sufficiently cooked, the skin is not only edible but tasty.

Enough for four.

Pickle Curries

Pickle curries are made in India and the Far East because they will keep for a fortnight, in the hottest weather—though not as long as pickles. No more than a dessertspoon of pickle curry should be eaten with curry and rice; the beginner should start with half a teaspoon or so and proceed gingerly.

SALTED LIME CURRY

20 limes cut open and well impregnated with salt. If limes are unobtainable, 15 lemons will do instead	1 stick saffron or turmeric
	8 pods garlic
	1 doz. green chillis
	4 tablespoons mustard oil

25 dried chillis—(red)	1 tablespoon ground mustard
1 dessertspoon of *maythi* (fenugreek)	5 breakfast cups of vinegar
1 teaspoon cummin seed	6 curry leaves
1 teaspoon mustard seed	salt to taste

Broil the dried chillis, fenugreek, mustard seed and cummin for 5 minutes, then powder finely. Also powder the saffron or turmeric. Halve each lime; peel the garlic; slit the green chillis lengthwise. Heat oil in the thick pan and put in the ground mustard and curry leaves. Add pounded curry spices, salt and other spiced ingredients; next the limes (or lemons), finally the vinegar. Bring gently to the boil, and simmer. When the liquid is thick and the oil clear on top (not frothy), the pickle curry is ready. Allow it to cool and put it into jars. Seal with *cork*, not metal, stoppers.

Salted lime curry is very, very pungent. The beginner should be warned to try not more than half a teaspoonful with curry and rice, and to take just a pinch with each mouthful.

As you grow accustomed to eating curries, you will like them hotter; though some (I am one) never grow to like very hot curries. They are an acquired taste—like whisky.

VINDE AULY

Vinde Auly is merely one kind of *vindaloo* or *bindaloo*, of which there are innumerable varieties. Vinde Auly, because it is made from pork, is rarely met in the Muslim North and North-West, but is a favourite in the South. It is a relish rather than a main dish, though a satisfying and tasty meal can be made of vinde auly and rice alone.

2 lb. salt pork. This must be well and truly salted	1 piece of turmeric
30 large red, dried chillis	¾ teaspoon of ground mustard
1½ heaped teaspoons of powdered cummin	1 pod garlic (comprising many cloves or segments)
	½ pint vinegar

Cut the pork into large cubes and dry them in the sun all day. If there is no sun, this can be done in the oven, though you must take care only to dry them, and *not* cook them.

Cut up and soak chillis overnight in vinegar, mash them into a paste with the turmeric, cummin, mustard and garlic. Gradually pour vinegar from chillis into paste, mixing well. Put the concoction into a large glass jar with a wide mouth.

Gently plop the pieces of pork into the jar, and if the liquid does not cover the pieces, add vinegar until it does. Seal the jar with an airtight cork or stopper. After two days, see whether the liquid has been absorbed by the pork. If so, top with more vinegar.

When wanted, remove as many pieces as you need; just cover in water and boil. When the liquid thickens and the fat clears, it is ready to eat—warm—with curry and rice, chappattis and rice, with plain rice, or chappattis only.

PUDDA (South Indian relish)

2 lb. cod or similar fish
90 dried (red) chillis (why not 100?)
2 one-inch pieces of turmeric
1 pod of garlic (this contains many cloves)

2 dessertspoons cummin—powdered
1½ bottles vinegar
tamarind—the size of 4 ducks' eggs
salt

Clean and cut the fish into round slices, each about 1½″ thick. Rub well with salt and leave for two days. Fish will keep, even in India, if well salted. After that, wipe well with a clean cloth and put in the sun for two days. (This should be tried in midsummer in a year when the sun is less fickle than normal. The Meteorological Office should be consulted.)

Pound and make a fine paste of the chillis, turmeric, garlic, and cummin, using vinegar. Mix the tamarind and some vinegar, strain, and mix with paste. Add the remainder of the vinegar so that a gravy-like consistency is achieved. If too thick, add more vinegar.

Dip each slice of fish in this gravy and place in a wide-mouthed jar; or in more than one jar. Then pour the remaining gravy over the fish, and cover with an air-tight cork, or some other air-tight cover. In this way the fish keeps, even in the Indian summer—and not in a refrigerator! —for a month.

When wanted for consumption, remove a slice or two and fry on both sides in butter for a minute; then add some of the gravy and cook till soft. But never cook until the fish has soaked for 7 or 8 days. To be eaten with curry and rice.

CHAPTER EIGHT

Planning Menus with Indian Dishes

INDIAN meals are not planned on the same lines as they are in Europe today. In Indian households, lunch and dinner do not usually start with soup or *hors-d'œuvres*. The appetite does not need whetting; the smell of the curries does that.

And—there is no breakfast in the British sense, even though Englishmen abroad insist on grapefruit, bacon and eggs, porridge and cream, marmalade and toast, followed by tea or coffee. Indians in the North break their fast with tea or water, in the South with coffee; this is followed by either a little fresh fruit or something light, like *falowries* or *bhajias*.

The vast mass of the population eats little throughout the day: a snack of curry and rice, or curry and chappattis, and water, sherbet or tea. Afternoon tea is an English meal, now copied by millions, which consists of biscuits, tea and Indian sweetmeats rather than the cakes, sandwiches and cress of the English. Cakes, biscuits and leaven bread were introduced by Europeans. The main meal in India is dinner, usually taken at a much later hour than in Britain, often about midnight.

Lentils and mulligatawny are never eaten as soups, but with rice and meat or vegetables. Lentils are cooked in a number of ways and eaten with rice or chappattis, often forming the most nutritious part of the meal. In the South, mulligatawny, which is a thin pepper water (described in *Curries of India*) is eaten with rice and sometimes accompanied by dry curries. The lentil and mulligatawny soups eaten at the start of a meal in Britain are adaptations from Indian cuisine—and there is no reason why Indian dishes should not be adapted. Below you will find a day's menus based on Indian food.

Breakfast:

Half a grapefruit, or a slice of melon or papaiya, a fruit which will soon become popular in England. Porridge or other breakfast cereal; or/and bacon and egg, toast and marmalade; tea, coffee or fruit juice.

Lunch:

Clear vegetable soup; vegetable or dhall curry accompanied by lime pickle or prawn sambal, followed by a slice of Madras hulva.

Tea:

This isn't, and never was, an Indian meal and the Indian sweets and savouries favoured do not, to the European palate, go well with tea. So, it would be safer to keep to sandwiches and pastries.

Dinner:

Soup (pumpkin, vermicelli, dhall, mulligatawny, mutton, chicken or rice soups); a fish curry made with coconut milk and eaten with bamboo pickle; or a white chicken curry with lime pickle; or pork or beef korma with bhurta and onion and tomato sambal; followed by a sweet of jellabies or kalajamoons, or rasagoollas with clotted cream. (Keep the sweet in the refrigerator till wanted.)

Curries may be eaten either with rice—plain or pilau—or chappattis.

Thumb through the recipes, concoct your own menus, but never serve more than two curries at any one meal. Curry and rice, or curry and chappattis, served with dhall, yogurt, bhurtas and sambals, and eaten with pickles, chutneys or chillis, are filling and substantial. If you serve too many curries your guests will be apt to overeat because the dishes are tasty, but they won't thank you.

The curse of the curry is that it is *too* tasty and the idea that the heat of the tropics dissuades one from eating too much is a fallacy. Tom Hopkinson describes in *In The Fiery Continent* some of the gargantuan meals eaten by well-to-do Africans. The same is true of Indians. Millions may be underfed, but those who can, too often stuff themselves, for obesity and strength are considered synonymous, and the saying, 'He is fat and strong,' is a compliment!

Meals Should Be Planned

Food as cooked by Indians who adhere to the *Code of Manu*, or abide by the Sustras, has a purpose, and meals should be planned, in much the same way as a menu is planned by a French chef. One dish should aid the next; and every dish should be complementary to all the others.

Thus a good Indian meal has design. Curry and rice should not be mixed together and eaten *en masse*. A little curry conveys richness and flavour; the blandness of rice assuages its pungency, and a *soupçon* of pickle gives it acidity, or chutney, sweetness.

A little food should be eaten at each mouthful; the mouth not plugged full—like a Scot filling his pipe with someone else's tobacco—and the whole should not be plunged madly down one's gullet as if one were starving.

Food should be well chewed, thoroughly tasted, and the many ingredients savoured and relished.

CHAPTER NINE

What Does One Drink with Curries?

ONE is often asked, 'What are the right wines to go with curries?'

In this the ancient books give no guidance whatever, for curries are indigenous to India, and India has no wines or spirits of her own except rum distilled in places like Shahjehanpur; arrack (Arabic, *sweet juice*) brewed in the country from the water of the coconut; and a potent liquor made from date-palm toddy (*tari*), all of which are shunned by the respectable, Hindu and Muslim alike.

Indians don't usually drink while eating, for if curries are too pungent, liquid does little to assuage the burning pangs. Rice or bread serves far better. Incidentally, long drinks after eating rice are not advisable, as they create a feeling of excessive fullness.

Sherbet

After a meal, when betel, cardamom and a little *paan* (a pungent leaf of the cress family) have been chewed to clean the teeth, sweeten breath and aid digestion, guests in India usually sip glasses of sherbet (Arabic *sharbah* from *shariba, to drink*; or Hindi *sharbat*) or cups of spiced tea.

Originally sherbet was made from fruit juice and snow, but today from any fruit juice, cooled and sweetened and with possibly a little rose water added. Indian sherbet bears no resemblance to the fizzy concoctions sold to children under that name in Britain. The most popular sherbets are made from mango, bael (wood apple), palm fruit, pineapple, lime, etc. Unfortunately, only the pineapple is available everywhere in Britain.

Spiced Teas

Spiced teas usually have a cinnamon, cardamom or mint base and are taken either hot or very cold, usually with sugar but never with milk. They contain herbs and are often flavoured with lime or lemon, and in a hot climate are very refreshing.

Wines, Spirits and Beers

When the Portuguese, French and British went to India they took their drinking habits with them, habits which were regarded as barbarous, for the orthodox Hindu does not touch alcoholic liquor, and the Prophet (whose name be blessed) forbids his followers to indulge in such delights. But today there are many Hindus and Moslems who place elastic interpretations on all such injunctions.

A good dry sherry goes well before dinner. Try one of the 'finos': a pale Amontillado or salty Manzanilla.

Generally speaking, light beers are the best beverages to drink with or after curries. The Japanese, a great rice-eating nation, drink *sake*, which is 15–18% alcohol and similar to sherry in flavour and strength, but light beers, like lager, are equally suitable.

Sweet, heavy red wines do not go well with curries; and if you want to drink wines, those like Riesling, Hock, Chablis, Sauterne, Graves or very dry sherries are best. Better far, I think, are perry or cider (sweet or dry), vintage cider, and, if you can run to it, after a very special occasion, a good champagne.

Perry is excellent with curries and I can't understand why more is not drunk. But this is merely a personal predilection.

There is, of course, no hard and fast rule about either eating or drinking in spite of everything Mr André L. Simon, Dr Saintsbury, Messrs Raymond Postgate or Cyril Ray might say. If you fancy a Guinness before, and a vintage port after your meal of curry and rice—and if it agrees with you—then to perdition with the Food and Wine Society!

Addresses of Curry Spice Suppliers

CURRY SPICES MAY BE OBTAINED BY POST FROM:

William Jones Ltd,
48/50 Bridge Street,
Chester

Fortnum & Mason Ltd,
181 Piccadilly,
London, W1

John Little & Son,
Eastgate Row,
Chester

Harrod's (Food Dept),
Knightsbridge,
London, SW1

A. Abdullah & Son,
2 Helmet Court,
London, EC2

Lal Jolly,
70 Warwick Road,
Earls Court, London, SW5

Army & Navy Stores,
105 Victoria Street,
London, SW1

Premier Supermarkets Ltd,
210–212 Earls Court Road,
London, SW5

The Bombay Emporium,
70 Grafton Way,
London, W1

Selfridge's (Food Stores),
Oxford Street,
London, W1

R. Brooks & Co.,
27 Maiden Lane,
London, WC2

Grimbly Hughes,
35 Queen Street,
Oxford

M. O. & E. A. Dell,
431 North End Road,
London, SW6

L. Palm (Delicatessen) Ltd,
The Market,
Oxford

Dell & Holt Ltd,
33 Tachbrook Street,
London, SW1

Cottle Brothers,
20/22 Queen Victoria Street,
Reading

Percy C. Richardson & Sons,
33a Brigstock Road,
Thornton Heath,
Surrey

Index